The Throws and Take-downs of

Greco-Roman Wrestling

Geoff Thompson

Copyright © Geoff Thompson 2001

All rights reserved. The right of Geoff Thompson to be identified as the author of this work has been asserted in accordance with the Copyright, Designs and Patents Act of 1988.

No part of this book may be reproduced by any means, nor translated into a machine language, without the written permission of the publisher.

Summersdale Publishers Ltd
46 West Street
Chichester
West Sussex
PO19 1RP
United Kingdom

www.summersdale.com

Printed and bound in Great Britain by 4edge Ltd, Hockley.

ISBN 1 84024 029 6

First edit by Kerry Thompson.

Photographs by David W. Monks, member of the Master Photographers' Association
Snappy Snaps Portrait Studio
7 Cross Cheaping
Coventry
CV1 1HF

Important note

If you have or believe you may have a medical condition the techniques outlined in this book should not be attempted without first consulting your doctor. Some of the techniques in this book require a high level of fitness and suppleness and should not be attempted by someone lacking such fitness. The author and the publishers cannot accept any responsibility for any proceedings or prosecutions brought or instituted against any person or body as a result of the use or misuse of any techniques described in this book or any loss, injury or damage caused thereby.

About the author

Geoff Thompson has written over 20 books and is known worldwide for his bestselling autobiography, *Watch My Back*, about his nine years working as a nightclub doorman. He currently has a quarter of a million books in print. He holds the rank of 6th Dan black belt in Japanese karate, 1st Dan in judo and is also qualified to senior instructor level in various other forms of wrestling and martial arts. He has several scripts for stage and screen in development with Destiny Films.

He has published articles for *GQ* magazine, and has also been featured in *FHM*, *Maxim*, *Arena*, *Front* and *Loaded* magazines, and has appeared many times on mainstream television.
Geoff is currently a contributing editor for *Men's Fitness* magazine.

Geoff was trained to instructor level at Greco-Roman Wrestling by USA Greco all-state champion Kris Wheelan.

Thank you to Jim Ault and all the members of the Birmingham Wrestling Club, also a big thanks to Kris Wheelan.

For a free colour brochure of Geoff Thompson's
books and videos please ring the
24-hour hotline on 02476 431100 or write to:

Geoff Thompson Ltd
PO Box 307
Coventry
CV3 2YP

www.geoffthompson.com
www.summersdale.com

Contents

Introduction — 10

Chapter One: Balance, Stance, Grip — 18

Chapter Two: The Snatch — 34

Chapter Three: Belly to Belly Suplex — 44

Chapter Four: Belly to Side Suplex — 49

Chapter Five: Belly to Back Suplex — 56

Chapter Six: The High Double Leg Take-down — 61

Chapter Seven: The Twisting Body-lock Take-down — 66

Chapter Eight: The Double Under-hook Lateral Drop — 72

Chapter Nine: The High Double Leg Hip Swing — 75

Chapter Ten: Off-balancing From the Body-lock — 79

Chapter Eleven: Head and Arm Take-down — 81

Conclusion — 86

Greco-Roman Wrestling

Introduction

The first time I experienced Greco was under the watchful and expert eye of master wrestler Kris Wheelan, my very good friend from the USA. I'd been training in freestyle at Birmingham Wrestling Club under the auspices of Jim Ault and had expressed an interest in this somewhat forgotten art. He suggested that I travel to Manchester, to the wrestling academy there, and train under Mr. Wheelan who would take me through a level one instructor course. Normally when I study an art I find myself sifting through the material offered and thinking, 'Would this work in a real fight?' Normally I am disappointed by what I see and end up disregarding up to 95 per cent of the material on offer. Whilst a lot of it may be practical within the periphery of a sport, or even the dojo, it doesn't normally stand up to what I believe and know to be the pressure of a real encounter in the street. Not so with Greco. When I first encountered the techniques on offer my initial thought was not the usual 'Will this work?' rather it was, 'These techniques are scary! Do I really want to learn something that has the potential to break necks and split spines?' It was frightening and so applicable to a real encounter.

Introduction

So it is with these words of warning that I offer this text as a reference book only. Some of the movements involved are recommended only under the tightest supervision. Join a good club and learn under the watchful eye of an expert.

Grappling, as I am sure you are aware, is the current flavour. In the martial arts everyone and their dog is enlisting in grappling classes in their bid to become the next Rigan Machado or Gracie. And in that sense I don't blame them. I was one of the many who fell under a similar spell in the seventies when a Bruce Lee film hit the screen and started a martial avalanche, the effects of which are still being felt some thirty years on. They say that things come in cycles, and it's true. The last time real wrestling was this popular was at the beginning of the century, between 1898 and 1914, when some of the greatest athletes in history donned their wrestler trunks and took their place in the Golden Age of Wrestling. The Great War was probably responsible for its early demise. Since that time it appears that grappling has almost disappeared from the public gaze. Judo was still there of course but, for some reason, people didn't see judo as the potent art it really is. They mistakenly thought of it as merely a sport. For those

Greco-Roman Wrestling

of us who have practised the art of judo we know better. I'd go as far as to say that judo is the best kept secret in the martial arts. But we were talking about wrestling (I see them all as wrestling, some jacketed and some not) and specifically the Golden Age where people like George Hackenschmidt (primarily a Greco fighter) brought this often maligned art to the world stage. Then there was Karl Pojelo of course, another great Greco fighter who was invited to America by President Eisenhower to test his wares against six of the top Japanese karate exponents of the time. Pojelo took each of them on in succession, and using only his wrestling skills he beat them all within minutes.

For those in the know the grappling arts have always been held in awe, the uninitiated are just catching up. Why are people suddenly catching on? Well, I've been trying to plug the cross training in Britain for the last ten years, and hopefully people like myself, Peter Consterdine and Rick Young have contributed to the renaissance, but it was the introduction of wrestling via the UFC (Ultimate Fight Competition – cage fighting, reality combat and extreme fighting) that really caught the imagination of the martial arts world. After one viewing

Introduction

of the Gracies (a legendary ju-jitsu family from Brazil, now residing in the USA) taking on opponents from every and any system and beating them almost effortlessly, everybody suddenly wanted to start a grappling class. Which is great, but unfortunately they did so to the detriment of their own arts and other valuable, nay vital ranges (and not unlike the Kung-Fu craze in the seventies and the Ninjitsu craze in the eighties). I can understand this to a degree, ground grappling has been missing from martial arts for so long, and the UFC type tournaments advertise grappling supremacy so well that it is natural that people should be drawn to it.

My time as a nightclub doorman taught me the necessity of close range grappling. From my first night on the pavement arena I knew how vital grappling was as a part of the martial armoury. You notice that I say 'as a part' and not 'as a whole.' Grappling is a vital means to an end but is not the end in itself. This is where the problems begin. Whilst it is important, even imperative, to include grappling on the curriculum it should not be to the detriment of the other ranges. With the advent of reality fighting, shoot and vale tudo, martial artists are leaving behind all their hard earned base to pursue a

Greco-Roman Wrestling

knowledge of grappling, most are abandoning their other disciplines, such as punching and kicking, to concentrate all their time and energy on the art of floor fighting. Not good if your intention is self-defence because outside the chippy, where the arena is concrete and the opponents come in groups, and armed, the floor is absolutely the last, and the wrong place to take a fight. A good 3-second fighter or an ambush fighter will take most trained fighters out of the game – no matter how good their ground fighting – before they are even aware that there was a game. And the fellow that goes to ground to take a strangle will likely get his head kicked in by the mates of his opponent. It is an arena that does not tolerate mistakes. So I think that it is vital to keep things in context when you practise Greco, or any art, it is just a part of the jigsaw; it is not the whole picture.

The main reason that I decided to write this series of books and make the instructional videos on throws and take-downs is because people are going mad for ground fighting, but they are taking little or no notice of how to get to the ground in the first place. You don't just end up there. You are either thrown down, dragged down, kicked down, or (if you are in

Introduction

charge of the affray) perhaps you have thrown your opponent to the floor. Much of what happens on the floor is dictated by how you got there in the first place. If you got there because you were knocked or thrown there it is entirely probable that your opponent will be in a position to stand back up and kick your head in. Or he may stay on the floor and, with no training at all in the martial arts, bite your ear or nose off. Do you practise these techniques in your dojo? Or do you, like most, start from a neutral position and disallow biting, butting, blinding and buddies (multiple attackers)? Normally, in the dojo scenario, both fighters are given an equal start; in a real situation there is no such neutrality and you very much have to make the best of what you are given, that is unless you are the one who controls the take-down (and this is my point and the reason for this book).

If you control the take-down then you get to control the ground (or not, if you decide not to hit the deck and run like the wind blows, as Forest Gump says). All of my ground fighting, both in and out of the dojo, is wholly determined by my standing work. I take people over with simple throw, like the ones in this text, and then, in transition from standing to

Greco-Roman Wrestling

ground, secure my position as soon as we hit the floor. Once I get the advantage – which the throw allows me to do – I never let my opponent back into the fight. It is also easier to attack on the floor than it is to defend. So it is vital that you get the throws off. The rule of thumb is that your groundwork is only as good as your standing. In this volume we will look at the throws and take-downs of Greco-Roman wrestling, of all the throwing arts this one is my favourite and, I believe, the most applicable for the street.

There was a lovely story about Bert Asarati, a great old wrestler from the fifties. After retiring from the ring Bert took to looking after nightclub doors for clubs in London. One night there was a terrible row and Bert was forced to use some of his wrestling skills (mostly Greco based), eventually flooring several would-be antagonists. One of the chaps he floored was unconscious for several hours and had to be taken to hospital where the police (who knew that Bert had done the damage) waited to interview him about the incident. When he finally regained consciousness looking groggy and sore the policeman said, 'What did Bert hit you with?'

Introduction

The fellow thought for a second then replied, 'Me mate, he hit me with me mate!' Apparently Mr Asarati had picked one guy up for a body-slam just as the other came into attack him so he hit the one fellow with the head of the other (ouch).

I digress. Having studied wrestling and made it work in live situations I can really vouch for this magnificent system.

As with any one range please don't make the throws and take-downs of Greco more than they are, it is only a small piece of the jigsaw.

The very best of good luck with your training and enjoy the book.

Greco-Roman Wrestling

Chapter One
Balance, Stance, Grip

Because Greco-Roman wrestling disallows any throw below the waist the players tend to stand a little higher then they would if they were practising freestyle wrestling, judo or sombo which does allow throws to the legs. Because they do not have to defend their legs from attack there is a tendency to be more vertical.

While fighting for a good grip the players usually work in a straddle-type stance, moving into the wedge position (left or right 45-degree stance) when setting up an attack.

Balance, Stance, Grip

Greco-Roman Wrestling

Presuming that you are working from a left lead stance (this can be reversed if you want to lead with your right) you should stand in a small 45-degree wedge stance, bent only slightly at the knees and relaxed, as illustrated.

Balance, Stance, Grip

In this position your weight is directly over a point just behind the heel of your front foot. The knees are flexed and your back is essentially upright and almost perpendicular to the floor. The head is up and in direct line with the spine. The shoulders are parallel to the floor.

The wedge stance gives you balance and offers a base from which you can throw or defend. It is important to maintain this stance if you want to stop yourself from being thrown. Never allow your feet to meet in the middle and don't over extend your stance. This will all come with mat practise. In the art of wrestling balance is everything.

Grip around the opponent's right triceps with your left hand and around the back of his neck with the right.

Greco-Roman Wrestling

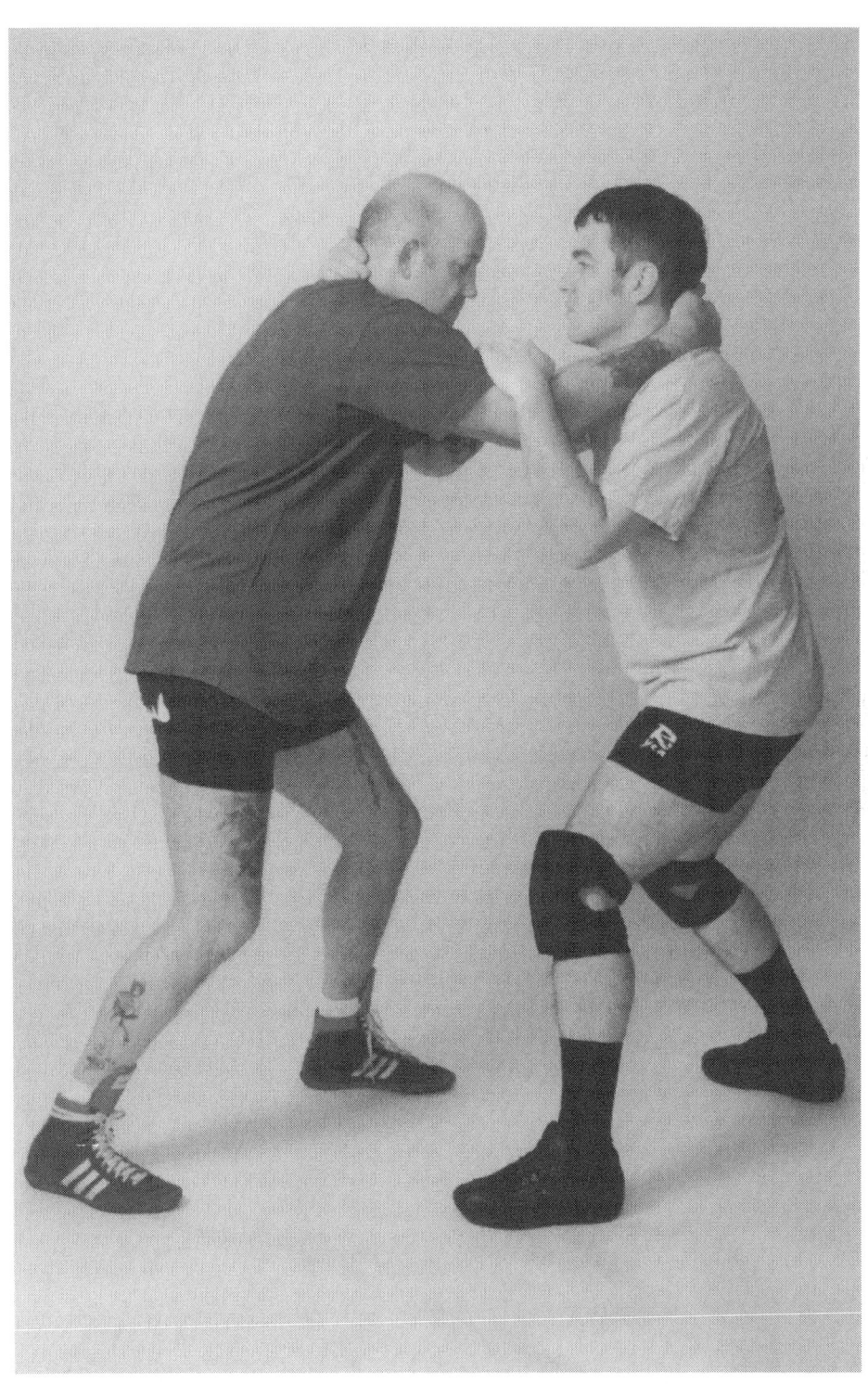

Balance, Stance, Grip

This is the basic stance and grip to take when looking for a throw. When entering for a throw the grip will change accordingly. This is a very basic grip, a neutral grip that you share with your opponent.

The grips being described in this book are nothing more than basic and, depending upon how far you wish to take the art of grappling, grip work can go to really high levels. A good player always controls the grip in most grappling systems before he even thinks about attempting a throw. At high-level competition it is usually the better grip fighter that dominates and wins the day. Excellence in grip work also allows small players to completely dominate large players with lesser gripping ability. When I was training at Neil Adams' club I was getting battered every session purely because I was being out-gripped. Usually within minutes of fighting I'd be dominated and then thrown because my opponents would not only dominate grip, they also wouldn't let me get a grip at all. I can't tell you what a difference it made to my fighting when the grip concept finally fell into place. Even with international players I could hold my own because I could fight for grip. It may take time for it to come together, but when it does it'll all have been worth it.

Greco-Roman Wrestling

So for now we should be content with basic grip. In the street encounter the problem rarely arises, you are very unlikely to be meeting any trained grapplers in a street attack – you hope. You very much have to work with what you are given in this uncompromising arena. Once you are a good gripper though, no arena will be a problem. Good grippers, especially judo players on the international set, are so good they throw people over with their grip alone. When my instructor, Wayne Lakin, took his second Dan he hardly had to execute a throw, he was so strong in the grip he was literally pulling his opponents off their feet. Another of my friends, 'Judo Jim', has been known to snap his opponents' fingers with his grip release techniques. But that's another book; this text is more about getting the basics right.

Once we have the basic stance and grip we use it to break the opponent's balance. On a street level most fighters have terrible balance, they tend to come to the fight with little more than raw aggression (which is often all they need to win a fight) and bad intention (which is often enough to scare the poo out of their opponents). A player facing an opponent of equal skill is very unlikely to throw him at all without breaking balance first.

Balance, Stance, Grip

You can break the opponent's balance with pulling or pushing actions or by attempting or feigning one throw to set him up for another.

Balance breaking does not vary from one system of grappling to another, so forgive me if you have heard any of this before; it does stand repeating. You break the opponent's balance by pushing or pulling him to the left rear, directly behind, to the right rear or directly to his right or left. Alternatively you can pull the opponent directly towards you, to your left or right rear or directly to the right or left. You can also pull him downwards.

Any one of these actions will force the opponent to move, hopefully out of stance and off balance, and when he does you can execute a throw.

I have always been an attacking fighter, but I do know that a lot of people prefer defensive fighting. They wait until the opponent makes his move before they attack, taking the opponent off balance as he tries to execute a throw.

Greco-Roman Wrestling

Stiff Arming

Stiff armers tend to favour jacketed grappling (Judo, Sombo, etc.) but there can still be an element of it in wrestling.

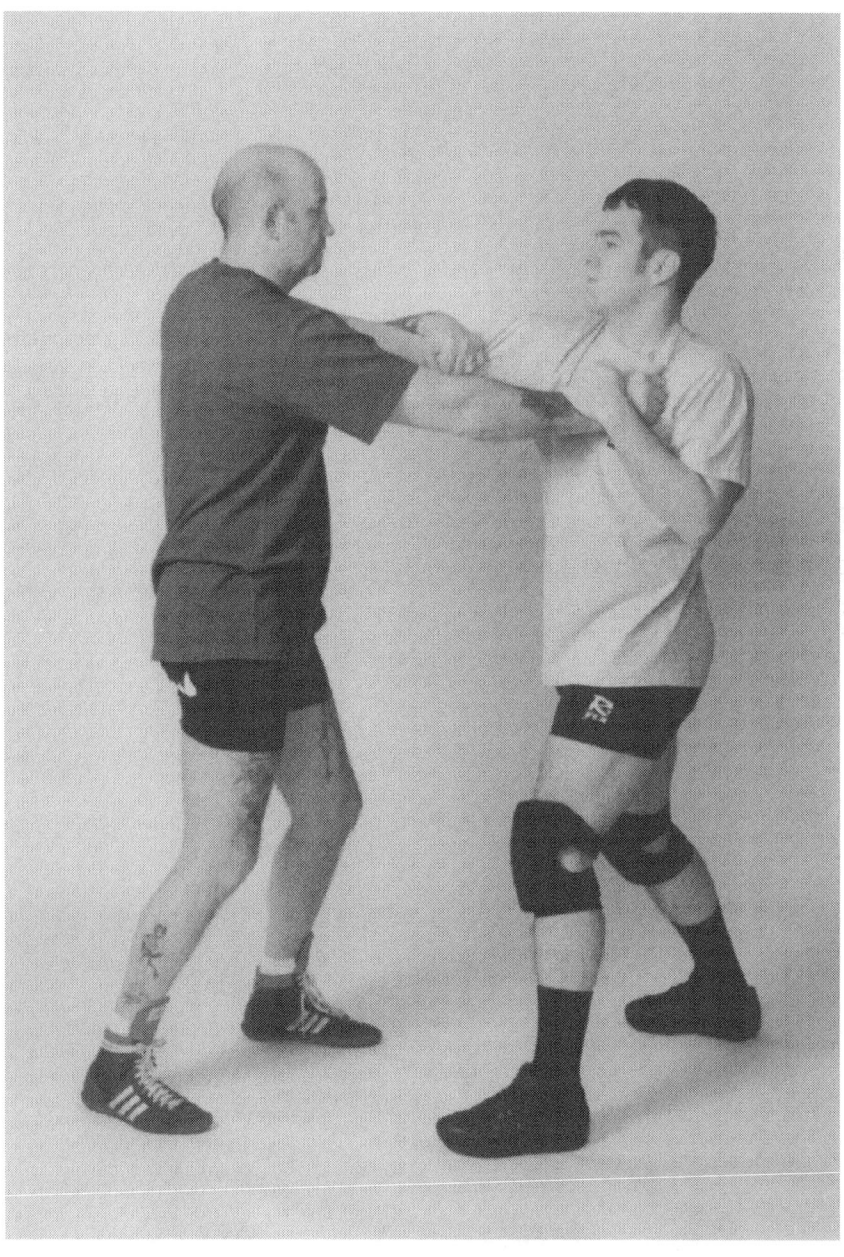

Balance, Stance, Grip

This phenomenon usually occurs with people who try to use strength over technique (never a good idea). Less skilful players, or nervy, scared players, especially the type that you will meet in a street encounter, will literally hold you to the spot with their strength. I have been stiff-armed (sounds painful I know) more times than I care to remember. In the street it's not really a problem because you just whack them and their attention is automatically drawn away from the grip; in the dojo however, just 'whacking them' might get you the throw but it will definitely lose you the contest because the referee will have you off the mat before you can say 'belly to belly suplex.' Stiff armers do little more than hold on for dear life, they don't attack or defend, they just hold. Dealing with them requires good grip work and a good sense of flow, using their strength against them by going with the flow of energy. If it's a street encounter, kick them in the 'reproduction kit,' or strike them with any available technique, before the throw. In days of old (when men were bold and . . .) this was legitimate, they called it 'blow before throw.' A strike as a precursor to a throw was a natural way to break an opponent's balance – both physical and mental – to set him up for the big throw.

Greco-Roman Wrestling

In the street you often encounter fighters with no clothing of any substance to grab; Greco and freestyle come into their own in these situations where you would need to revert to the wrestling hooks and holds to secure a take-down. Of all the grappling styles that I have studied this is one of the very best for the street because it relies totally on bodily control over an opponent using natural hooks. It also allows you, if the situation is favourable, to take a person over very gently without hurting him, or paradoxically (again if it was absolutely necessary), you could slam him hard into the floor and do a lot of damage. I like the idea of being able to control people without hurting them. Greco lets you do that.

Grips

Here are a few of the grips used in Freestyle and Greco-Roman wrestling.

Note: Never intertwine your fingers, when you try to pull them apart it is very easy to dislocate your fingers or knuckles.

Balance, Stance, Grip

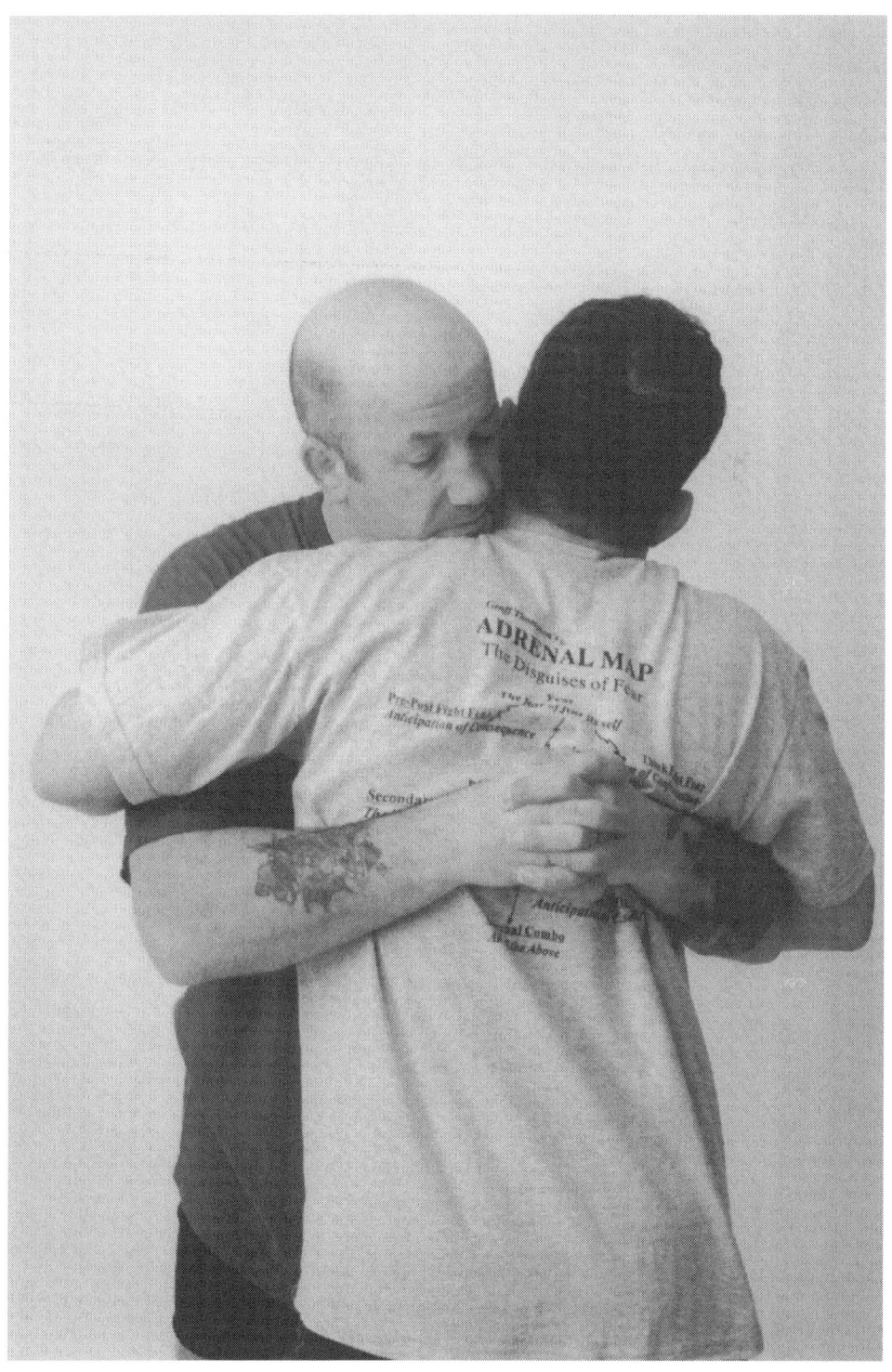

Greco-Roman Wrestling

Grab Finger Grip

Grab the four fingers of your left hand with the four fingers of your right hand. Lock them by closing your fists together firmly. Pull on all four fingers of both hands at the same time to ensure the lock.

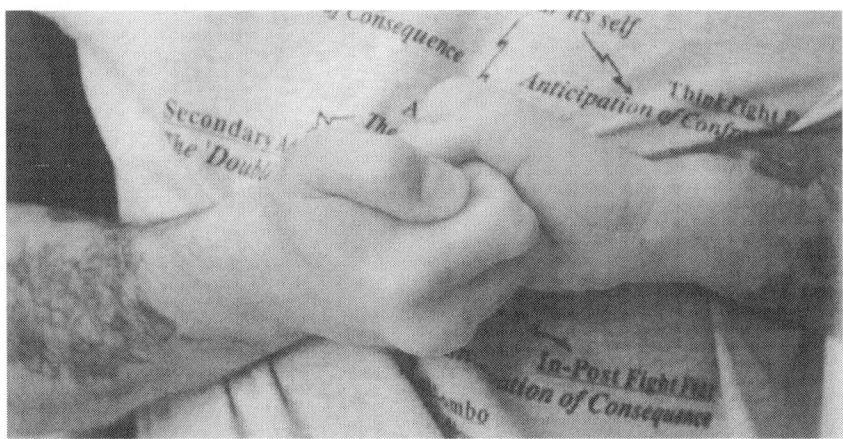

Wrist Grip

Grab your left wrist with your right hand (or vice versa) with your thumb and forefinger around your left wrist.

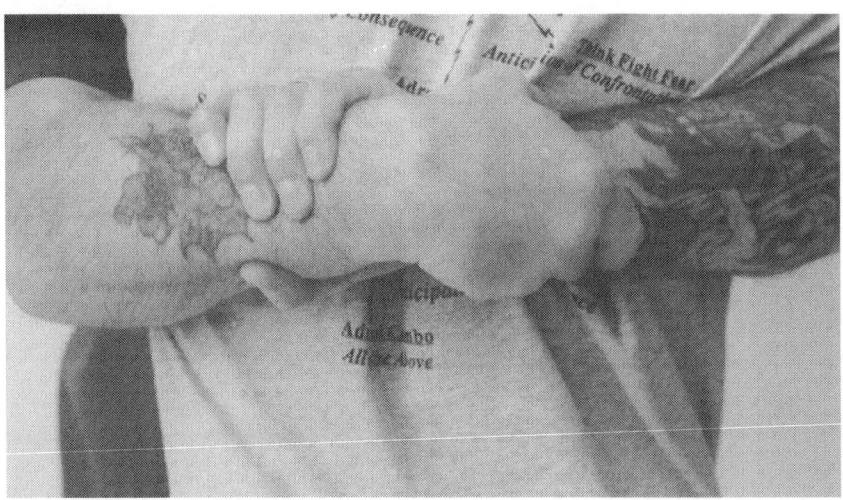

Balance, Stance, Grip

Grab Back of Hand and Wrist

Grab the blade side of your left wrist with your right hand. Your two smallest fingers should be around the wrist, the bigger fingers on the blade side of the hand. Your thumb should be on the same side as the fingers.

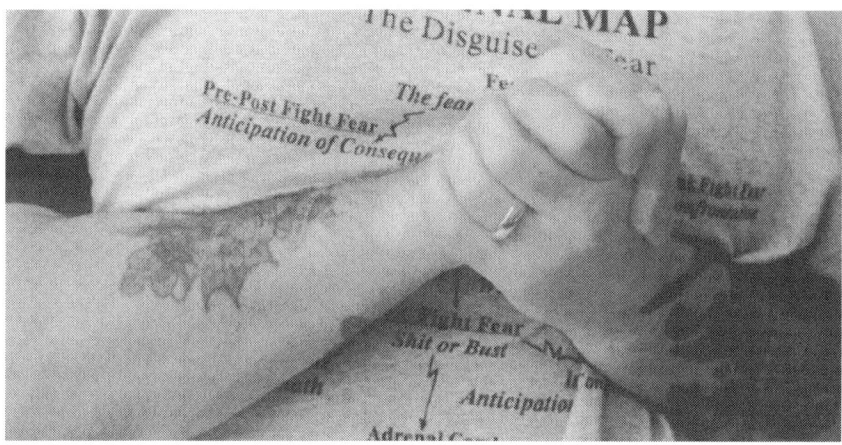

Palm to Palm Grip

Place your left palm on your right palm and clasp both hands around each other. (Shown with thumb in & thumb out.)

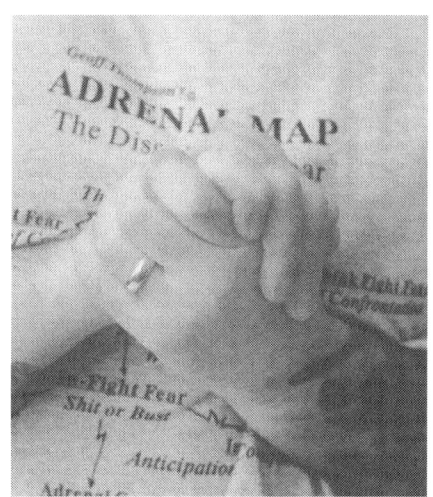
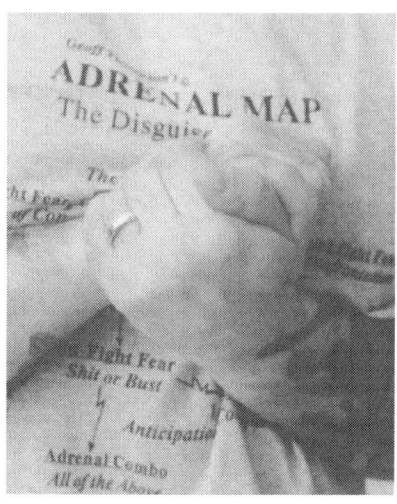

Greco-Roman Wrestling

Palm to Bicep Grip

Grab your right bicep with your left hand; bend the left arm to make the grip or lock strong. This lock is used especially for face or arm bars.

Balance, Stance, Grip

Put these grips into practise because they are the most important part of the take-down. No grip, no throw. To be honest the grip is the most exciting part of the fight to me, I love it. I know that from the outside it can all look a bit dull, it might look like nothing is happening when the players fight for grip, but when you know what you are looking at you'll love it. It's like a physical game of chess. And the power you feel once you understand and can use the grips. You get hold of people and they struggle to breathe let alone escape. It's a fantastic part of grappling that I urge you not to overlook.

Greco-Roman Wrestling

Chapter Two
The Snatch

Of all the Greco throws this one is probably my favourite. It doesn't look pretty, it isn't a devastating fall but it is very simple and very functional. Outside it works like a charm. Personally I couldn't give a monkey's bum what the throw looks like as long as it is functional, as long as it's potent. My old friend Dave Turton always told me that it didn't matter what colour the cat was as long as it killed mice. Enough said.

From the conventional grip, left lead wedge stance, snatch the opponent's head forward as though you are trying to smash his face into the floor (actually I suppose that is what you are trying to do) as you simultaneously lunge backwards with your right (or left) reverse leg. Drive his face to the floor. The shock of the attack will take him off balance and over on to his belly. From here you can finish however you wish.

The Snatch

Greco-Roman Wrestling

The Snatch

Alternatively you can use the snatch to capture the opponent's head in a guillotine by snatching him forward in the same way. Instead of trying to yank him over with the snatch, pull his head under your right or left armpit and wrap the same arm, under and around his neck so that you have him in a headlock or choke. From here, sprawl your legs backwards and drag the opponent on to his knees. Finish, again, however you wish.

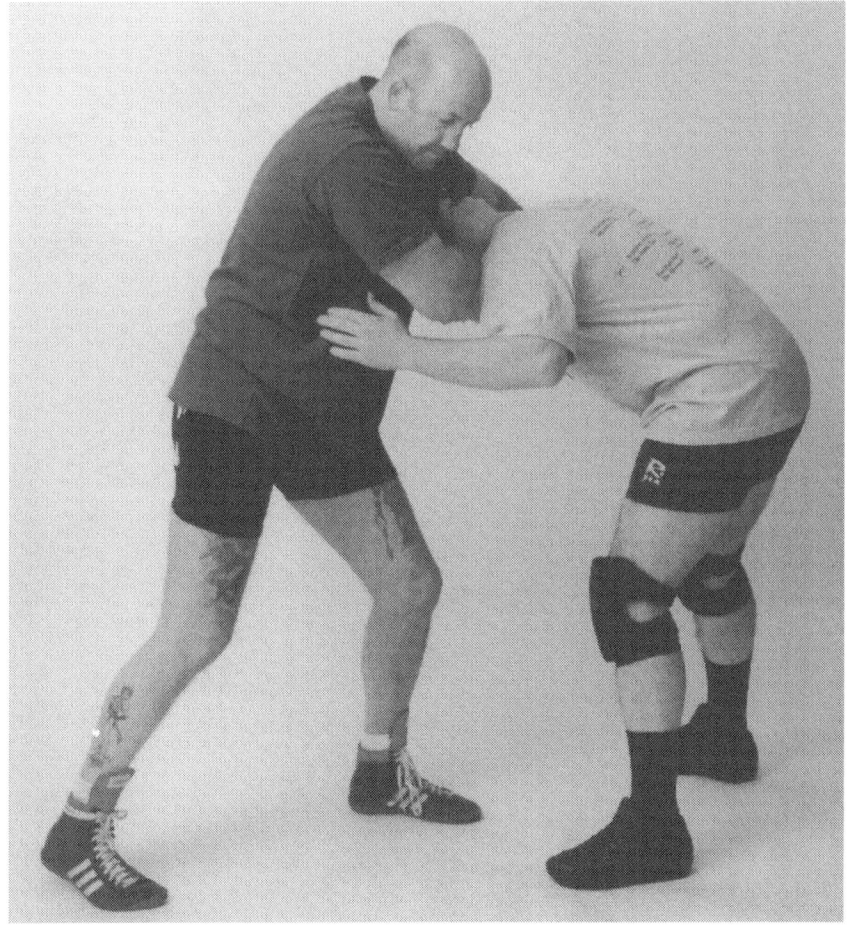

Greco-Roman Wrestling

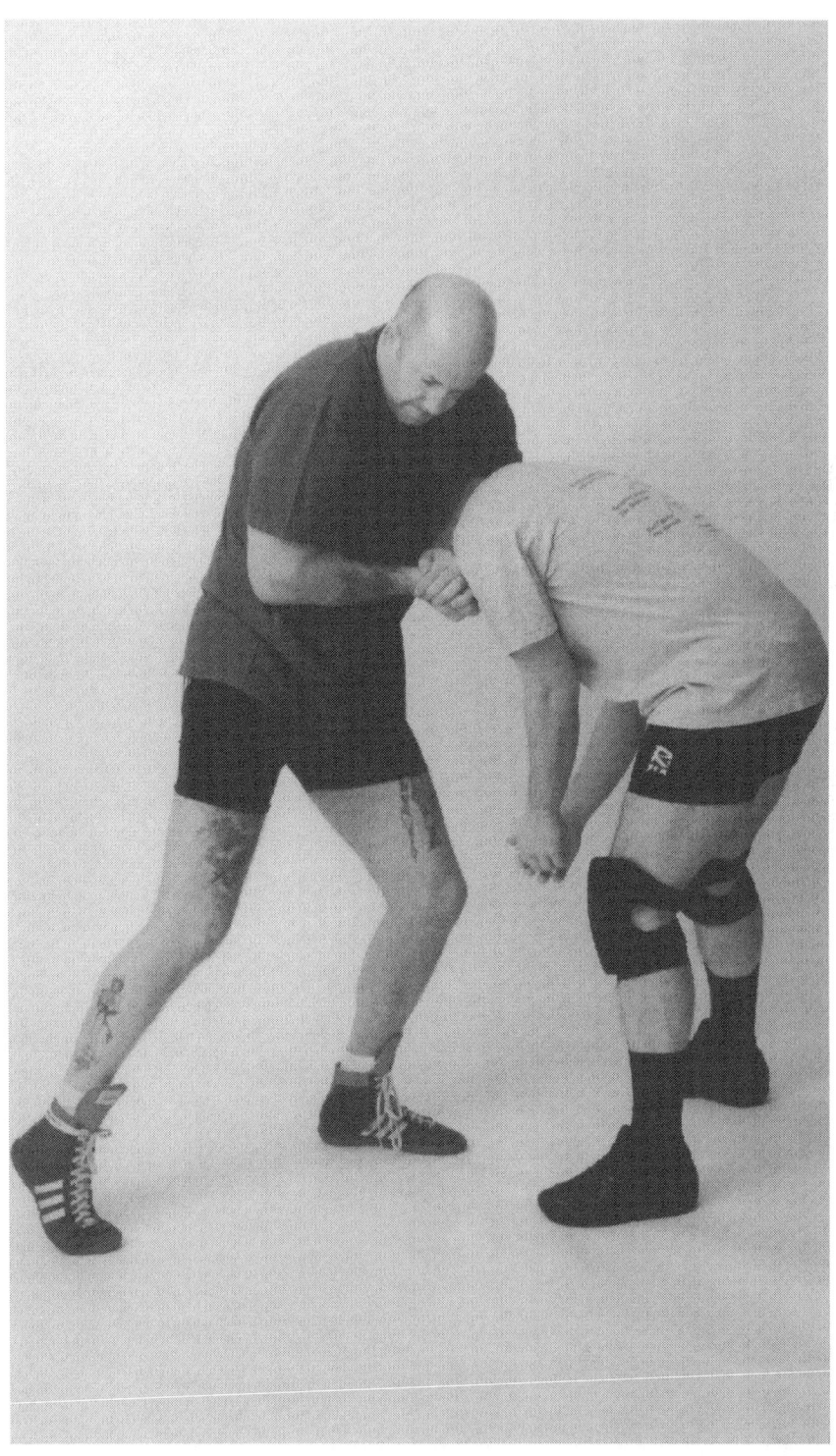

The Snatch

Yet another alternative from the snatch is to suplex the opponent over your head. Snatch the opponent forward and catch his head in a lock, step in close so that both of your feet are level with, and outside the opponent's feet. Bend very deeply at the knees keeping your back as straight as possible. You should be right underneath his centre of gravity. Pick him up by the head and throw him over your head by straightening your legs and arching your back, crab-like.

Greco-Roman Wrestling

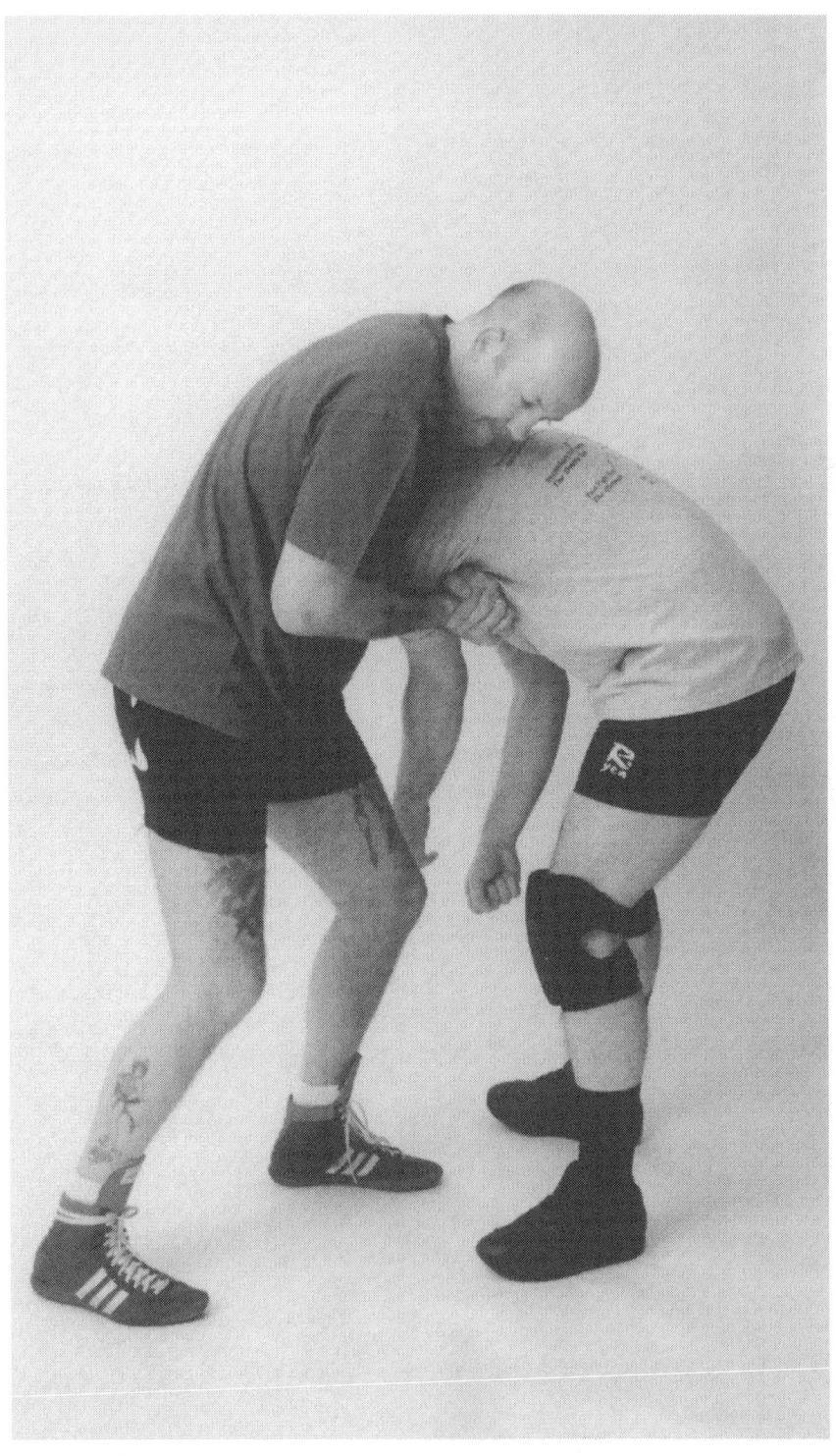

The Snatch

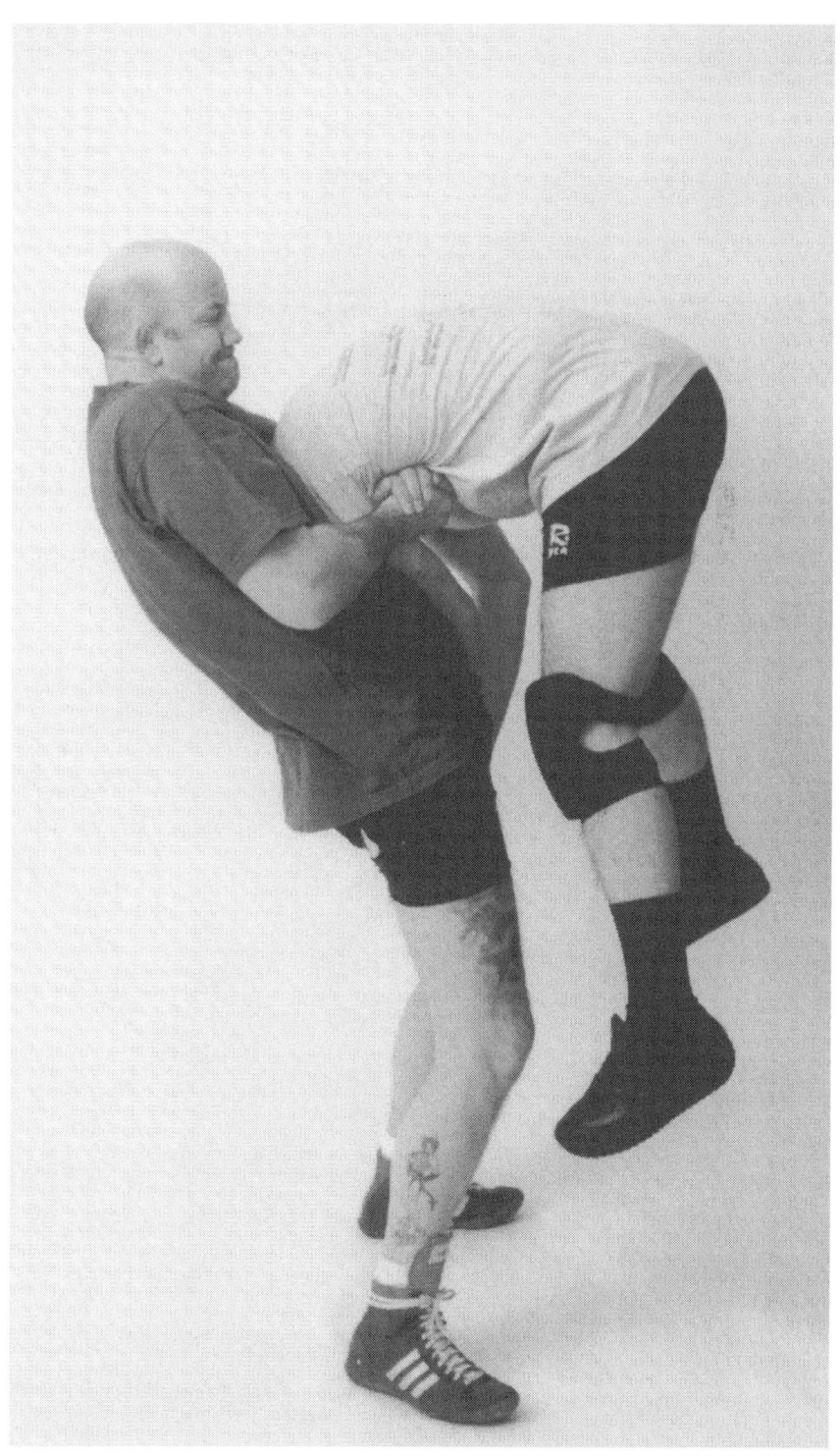

Greco-Roman Wrestling

Another alternative from the snatch is the same suplex via the opponent's waist as opposed to his head. Snatch the opponent's head forward so that he falls into you. As he does so reach over his back and wrap your arms around his waist. Step into him so that both of your feet are level with and outside the opponent's feet. Bend very deeply at the knees keeping your back as straight as possible. You should be right underneath his centre of gravity. Pick him up and throw him over your head by straightening your legs and arching your back, crab-like.

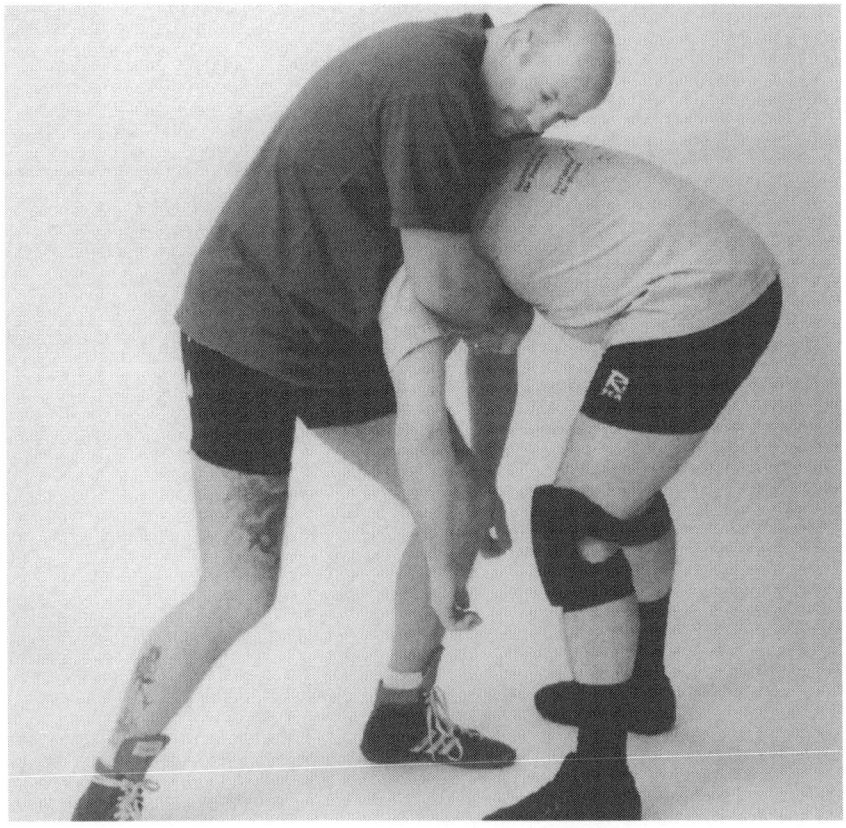

The Snatch

Greco-Roman Wrestling

Chapter Three
Belly to Belly Suplex

Of all the suplex throws I would say this has to be the most difficult. But, as with all the suplex throws, it does have an awesome effect on the opponent when you throw him clean over your head, especially in the street scenario.

Wrap your arms around the waist of the opponent and grip very tight at the small of his back (take any grip you can as long as it is very tight, your grip needs to be iron tight to keep him close enough to throw). Your bodies should be almost welded together. Any gaps at all and the throw will not happen. Drop your centre of gravity so that your legs are heavily bent and you are beneath his centre of gravity. Your feet should be at least parallel with his, even behind his. Depending upon where his feet are you can stand outside of them, inside of them or somewhere in between. Pick him up off the floor and throw him directly backwards and over your head by straightening your legs and arching your back, crab-like.

Belly to Belly Suplex

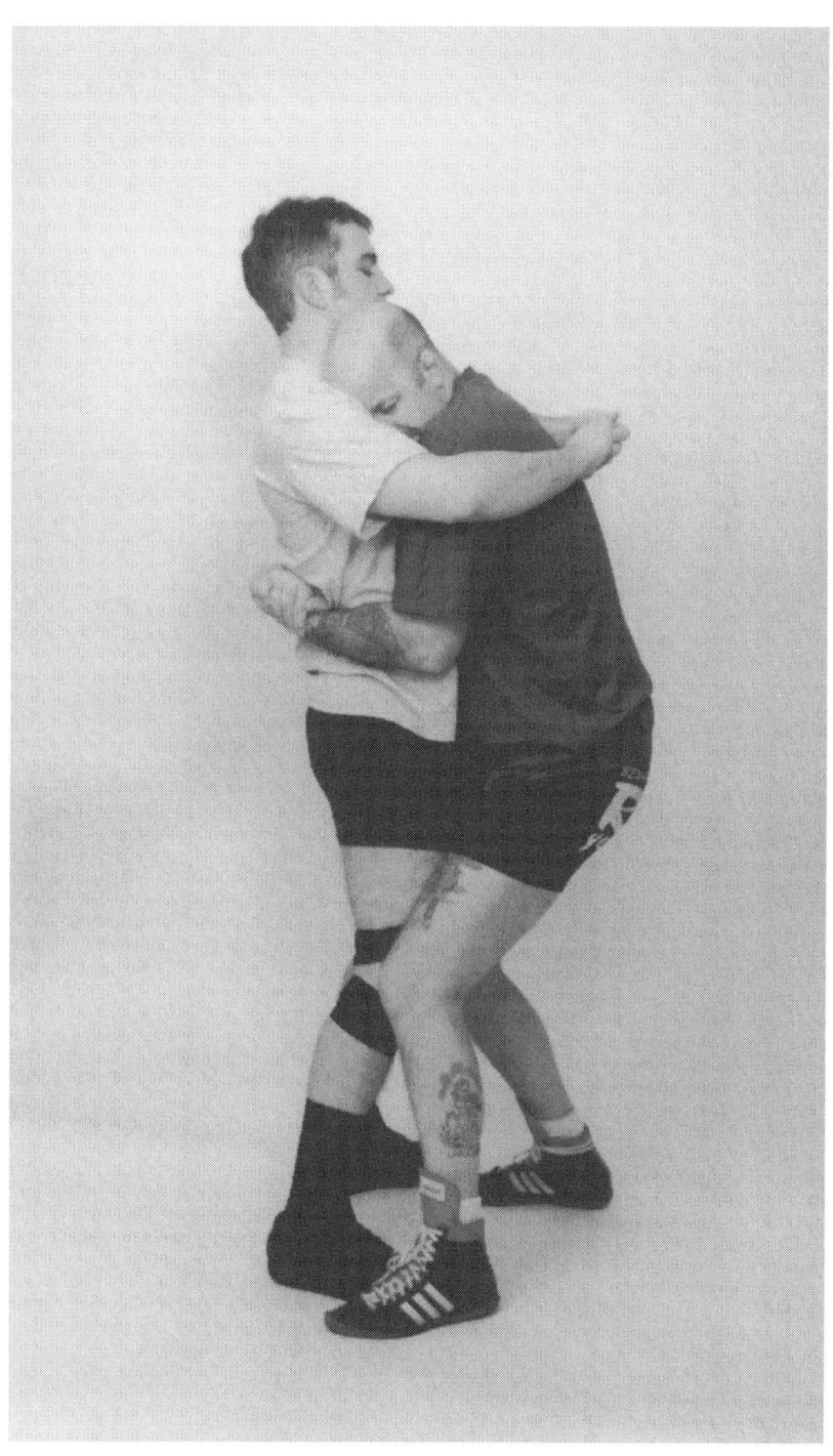

Greco-Roman Wrestling

At the end of the throw you have the option to turn just as the opponent is about to hit the deck (this would not then be a full suplex) or simply arch right into a crab position landing the opponent on his neck or head.

Belly to Belly Suplex

You can employ this throw by grabbing around the waist, or by grabbing around the opponent's arms or by entangling just one of his arms, as illustrated. As long as it allows your hands to meet and grip. As I said, the grip you take will vary according to where you take the grip and the girth of your opponent.

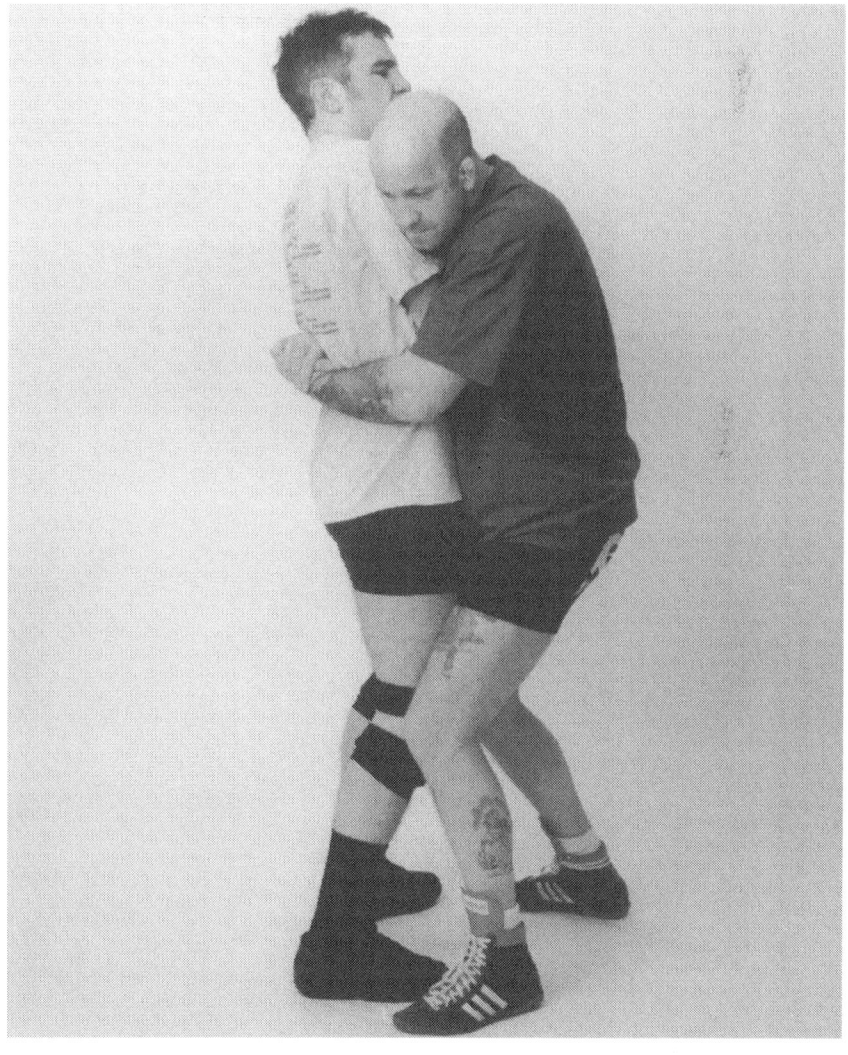

Greco-Roman Wrestling

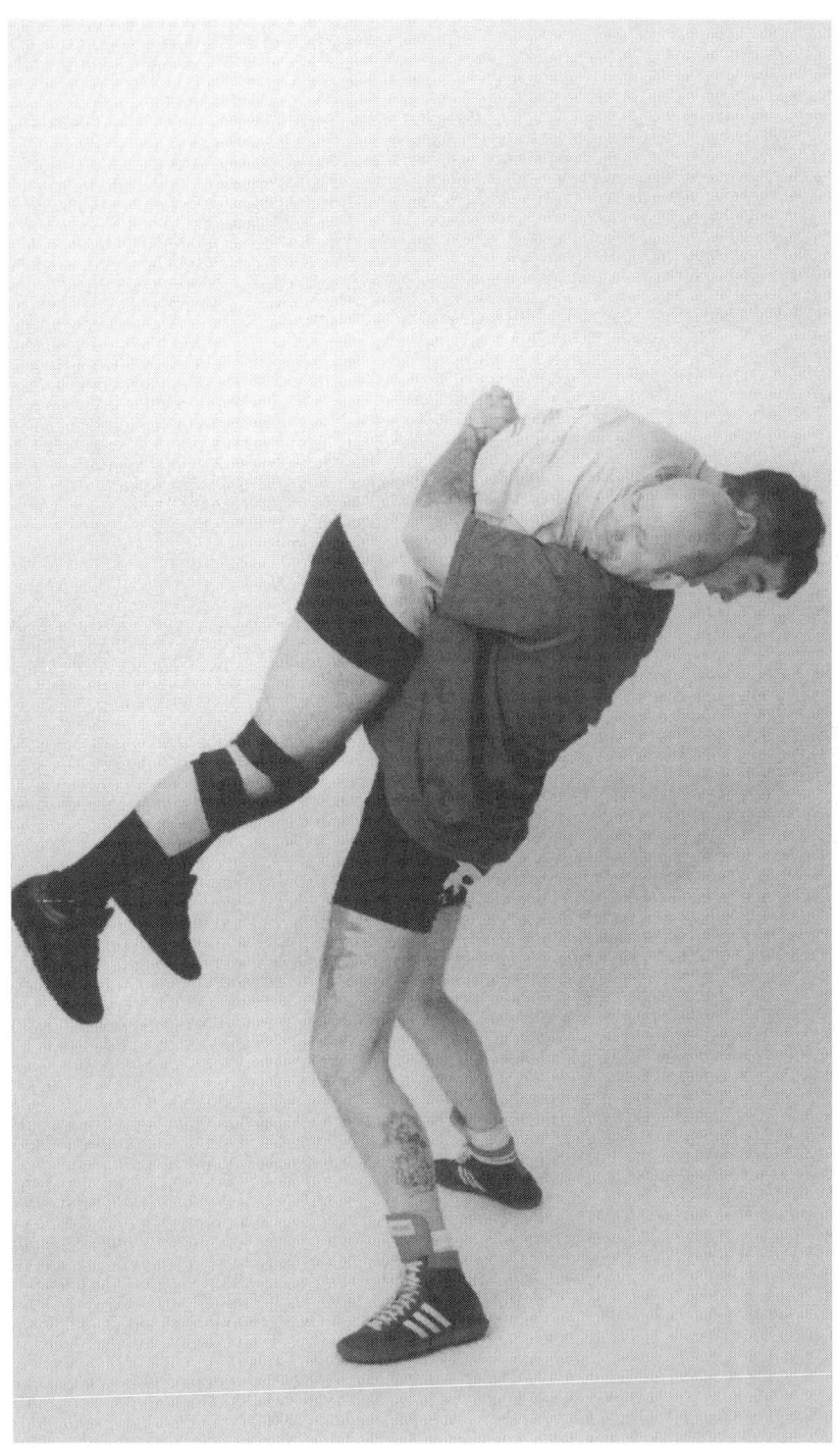

Chapter Four
Belly to Side Suplex

In actuality all suplex type throws are very similar, it is only the entry and where you grip that changes. So, in effect, as long as you can get both arms tightly around the opponent and join them at the other side you can suplex them. The counter to a suplex, if you get caught, is to either drop forward to the floor, in which case the opponent is where you want him anyway, or to hook your foot or feet, as shown.

Greco-Roman Wrestling

Hook your foot around the inside of the opponent's calves. If your opponent uses this defence you would counter by falling or pushing him forward so that you land on top of him, again getting him where you wanted him in the first place. With the belly to side suplex you can either take the throw simply because you have found yourself in the ideal position to do so or you can create a window, an entry, to set up the throw.

Let's have a look at how you would make the entry to take the throw.

As the opponent's right arm reaches to grip your left shoulder, hook around the opponent's wrist with the inside of your wrist and sweep it around and into his own side. You can if you wish use your right hand to grab and assist this motion, as illustrated. I always do. As you do so, step across the opponent's legs with your right leg and wrap your arms around his waist, joining at the small of his back while simultaneously trapping his right arm in the process. In the same smooth action, step around the back of his legs in a circular motion with your left leg and drop deep so that you

Belly to Side Suplex

are below his centre of gravity, pick the opponent up and suplex him over your head. At the end of the throw, as the opponent is hitting the floor, you have the choice of turning out of the arch or going into a crab position.

Greco-Roman Wrestling

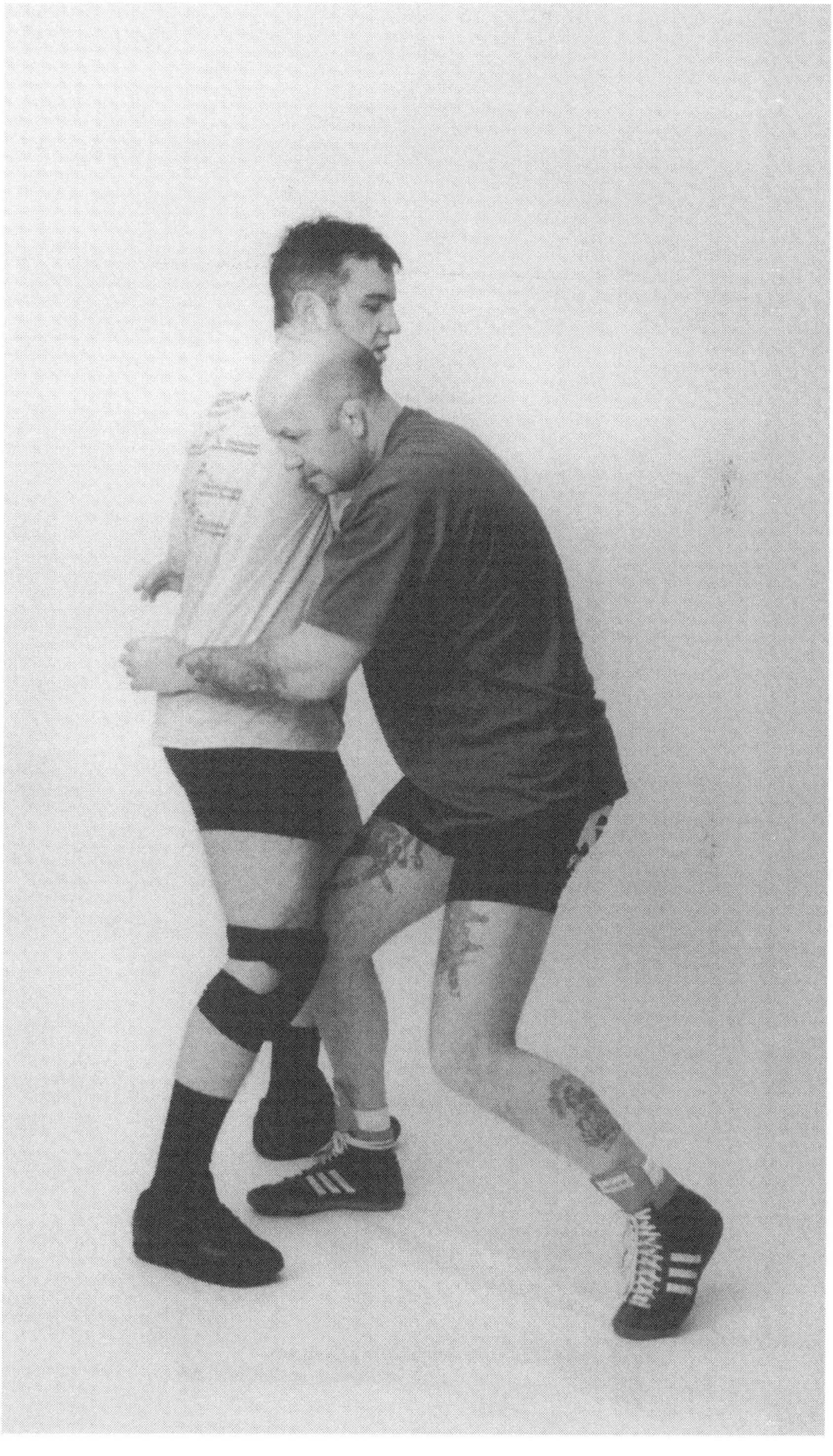

Belly to Side Suplex

Greco-Roman Wrestling

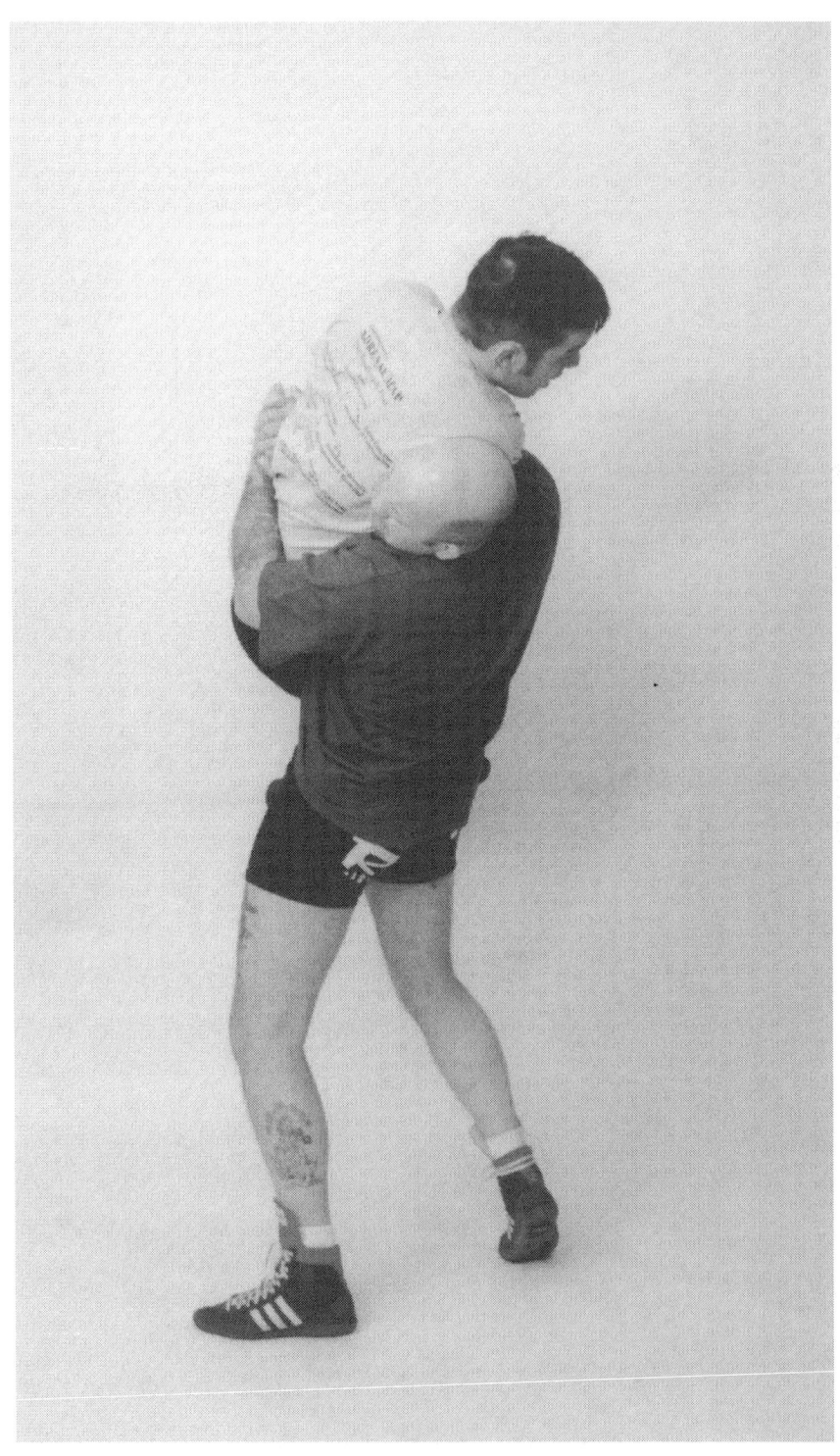

Belly to Side Suplex

This whole throw should be done smoothly and without hesitation, it should be one flowing action so that momentum aids you in the throw and the opponent has no time to block it.

The hand action at the beginning of the throw is complicated to start with, but gets easier with practise. My own Greco coach, Kris Wheelan from the USA, had us work on the entry to the throw independently of the throw itself. As with all throw and groundwork techniques it is the catch that is vitally important. Without that you haven't got a throw. So isolate the hand action and practise it thousands of time so that it comes as a natural reaction to any kind of grab. Important also is the lift itself. Try not to bend your back when executing the throw but bend at the knees and keep the back as straight as possible. The power in the suplex throw is in having a strong grip around the opponent's waist and driving from the legs. Once you have the throwing action off you will start finding the suplex from lots of different positions. Even when people make their entry for a throw you will find yourself picking them up and throwing them over your head.

Greco-Roman Wrestling

Chapter Five
Belly to Back Suplex

This is the most common of all the suplex throws and the one most demonstrated in wrestling (show and shoot) matches. I also find that it is the easiest of all the suplex throws because you are actually behind the opponent and therefore he cannot defend very much, other than to fall forward on to his knee, which is OK because he is on the floor where you wanted him in the first place.

Again it is the entry that is important here but of all the suplex throws the entry to this one is the easiest and the most natural. Very often when fighting, especially in the street scenario, you find yourself behind the opponent (though you won't quite know how you got there) but with no knowledge of what to do with the opportunity. In this case we will take the throw from an entry as opposed to just being behind the opponent.

You can do this in one of two ways: either duck under the arm of the opponent as he makes to grip you, then slide

Belly to Back Suplex

behind him, or simply duck under his grip once it has been taken and then slide behind him.

As the opponent tries to take a high grip on you, prop his right arm up with your left hand, as shown, and duck underneath it, keeping your head very close to his body.

Simultaneously step behind him with your left leg and allow your right arm to wrap around his waist. Once behind him turn so that your belly is to his back and join your right and left hands at his lower abdomen and squeeze very tight. Drop your weight at the knees so that you are below his centre of gravity and pick the opponent up. Suplex him over your head in the usual manner, arching your back as you throw.

Greco-Roman Wrestling

Belly to Back Suplex

Greco-Roman Wrestling

Again I must stipulate that the whole sequence of these throws must be smooth with no (or few) stopping and starting actions. Any stutter in the smoothness of the entry could allow the opponent an exit. Smoothness will only come from practising many times.

Chapter Six
The High Double Leg Take-down

This is a very similar throw to the low double leg take-down of freestyle wrestling. Of course in the Greco they do not allow any attacks to the leg area of the body (not that this would not affect you in the street scenario where the only rule is 'there are no rules'), so they take the throw higher up on the hips of the opponent.

Wrap your arms around the waist of the opponent. Make your grip (your grip depends upon how thick the opponent's waist is) at the small of his back, just above his hips. Simultaneously drop all your weight on to your right (or left) leg and drive your right (or left) knee to the floor between and just past the inside of his legs. Your left knee bends to the right side of his body and is used like a starting block to drive the opponent on to his back. Your head goes tight into his right side, just under his armpit. This whole action has to come together as one piece and you should explode into the opponent so that he has no time to defend.

Greco-Roman Wrestling

The High Double Leg Take-down

Greco-Roman Wrestling

An alternative to this technique is to attack exactly the same way only with both knees between the opponent's legs as opposed to one inside and one out. This can be quite effective if you have been pulled to your knees anyway, just wrap your arms around his waist and drive him over.

Wrap your arms around the waist of the opponent, on the inside of his arms (this would also work on the outside of his arms if you could trap them by his sides). Make your grip at the small of his back, just above his hips.

The High Double Leg Take-down

With both of these attacks there is the obvious danger of getting your head caught in a guillotine attack or a strong headlock. To avert this keep your head as tight into your opponent's body as it will go and keep you left shoulder high so that there are no gaps for him to take the headlock.

Greco-Roman Wrestling

Chapter Seven
The Twisting Body-lock Take-down

As a defence to the last throw the opponent may drop his body weight to disable your entry to the throw. If he does defend in this way your grip will naturally slide higher up his body so that your arms are under his armpits. In this instance you can take the opponent over with the twisting body lock. This doesn't necessarily have to come as a counter to the last defence. It is a legitimate throw in its own right and can be taken at any time as long as your arms are in the right position. As your arms come under the opponent's armpit step back with your left leg and thrust upward with your right arm, so that the opponent's left arm is forced up and over. By making small steps, keep moving in a circle (clockwise or anticlockwise depending upon which armpit you are under) and thrust the opponent's arm over so that he is forced off balance and on to his back.

The Twisting Body-lock Take-down

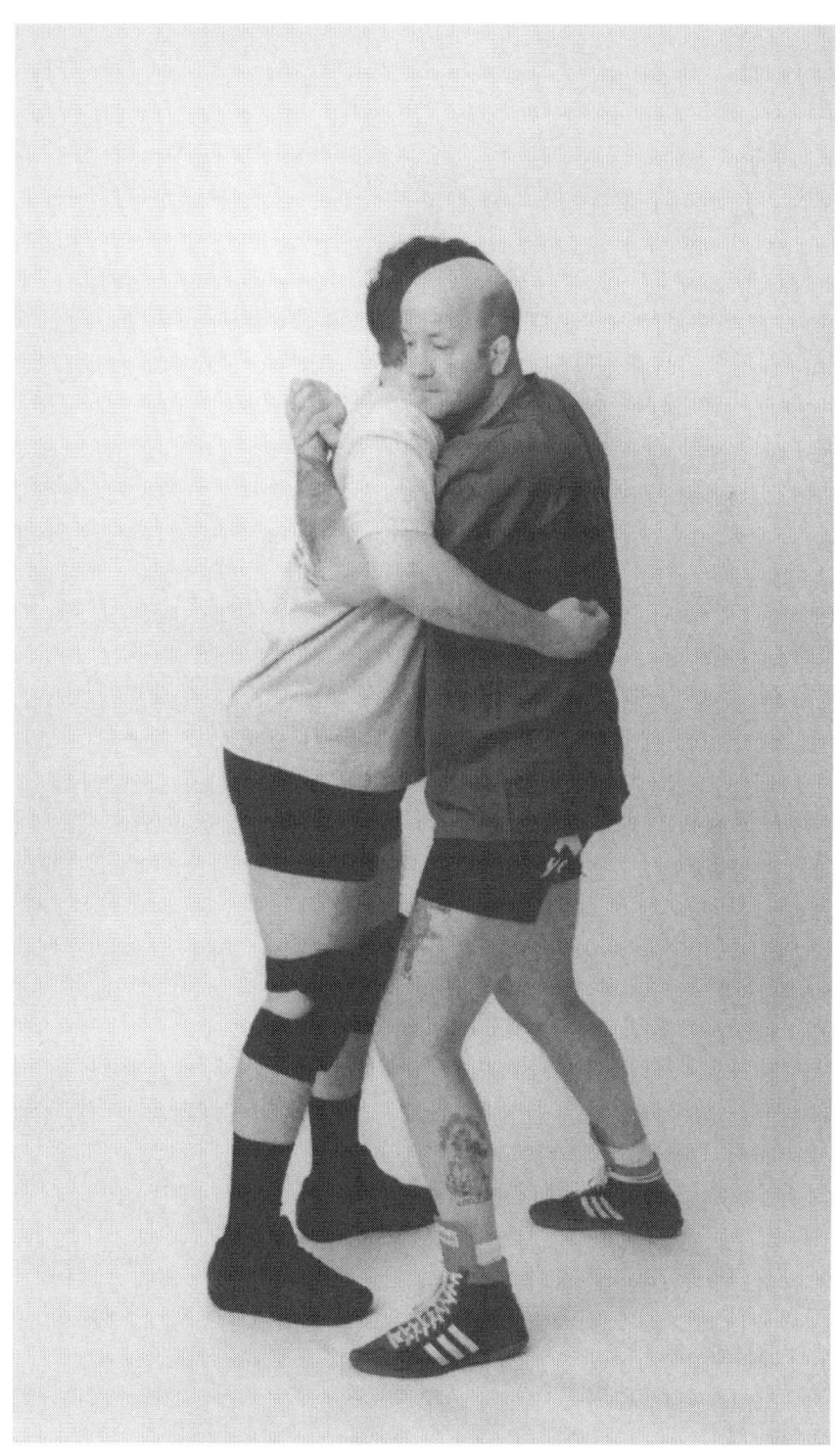

Greco-Roman Wrestling

The Twisting Body-lock Take-down

Greco-Roman Wrestling

Exactly the same throw can be taken effectively from the single under arm grip. Trap the opponent's right (or left) arm on the outside as you thrust his other arm, from under the armpit, up and over.

The Twisting Body-lock Take-down

Chapter Eight
The Double Under-hook Lateral Drop

This is very similar to the last few throws, working from the double under-hook, only this time the throw is almost a suplex.

Pull your opponent towards you and back-peddle so that he has to follow. When he is in a position so that he has one foot forward and one foot back, plant both of your feet close together so that the heels of your feet become the throwing base. As you pull him to you, swing him in the direction of the trailing foot and drop laterally so that he is falling on to you. As this occurs thrust your right thigh against his right thigh and twist in mid air so that he is turned on to his back and you on to your front, as illustrated.

The Double Under-hook Lateral Drop

Greco-Roman Wrestling

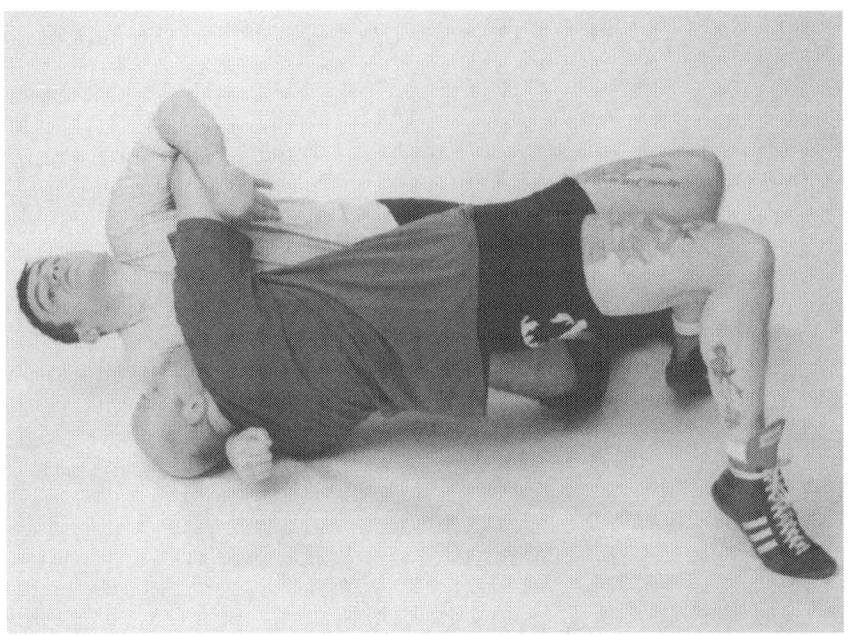

This is by no means an easy throw and it is very important that you practise initially on a crash mat so that neither you nor your opponent is hurt. It takes a lot of confidence to execute a throw like this and caution in practise is always recommended.

Chapter Nine
The High Double Leg Hip Swing

This is the kind of technique that the cage fighters, or shoot fighter in the UFC (Ultimate Fight Competition) like to employ because it doesn't expend a lot of energy and it allows you to keep control of the opponent once he has been taken to the floor. In a self-defence situation it would be more important to slam your assailant to the floor very hard so that you can make good an escape.

The entry to this throw is the same as that of the high double leg.

Wrap your arms tightly around the opponent's waist, so that you are belly to belly. Tuck your head tightly into his right chest or shoulder area. Place your right (or left) leg forward and between his legs. Drop your body at the knees and pick the opponent off the floor. When he is up hold him tightly to your body as you turn slowly. Move his hips so that he twists in the air and at this point drop him on to his back.

Greco-Roman Wrestling

The High Double Leg Hip Swing

Greco-Roman Wrestling

Again be very careful of getting your head caught in the opponent's headlock. He will try to grab your head in defence to the throw. Keep it very tight to his body so that there are no gaps for him to move, let alone take the headlock.

Chapter Ten
Off-Balancing From the Body-lock

From the body-lock position, arms wrapped tightly around the opponent's waist, join them at the small of his back. Drive your left leg between and behind his legs whilst forcing your weight to your left. As the opponent adjusts to keep his balance, drive forward and down taking his back to the floor.

Greco-Roman Wrestling

Again close body contact at all times is necessary for the throw to find effect; any gaps and you'll be unsuccessful.

Chapter Eleven
Head and Arm Take-down

This is another throw that takes control of the head to gain control of the body. As a rule of thumb this is very effective. Once you control the head of the opponent you also control the body. It is very hard for the body to resist once the head has been forced in a certain direction.

With the head and arm take-down you take charge of the opponent's head by forcing your right arm over his left shoulder and joining it with your left hand underneath his right armpit. Clasp the hands tightly together and step forward, quickly, to the outside of his right leg whilst forcing his head backwards with your right bicep. As his weight tumbles backwards, slam his back to the floor and follow through to a pin.

Greco-Roman Wrestling

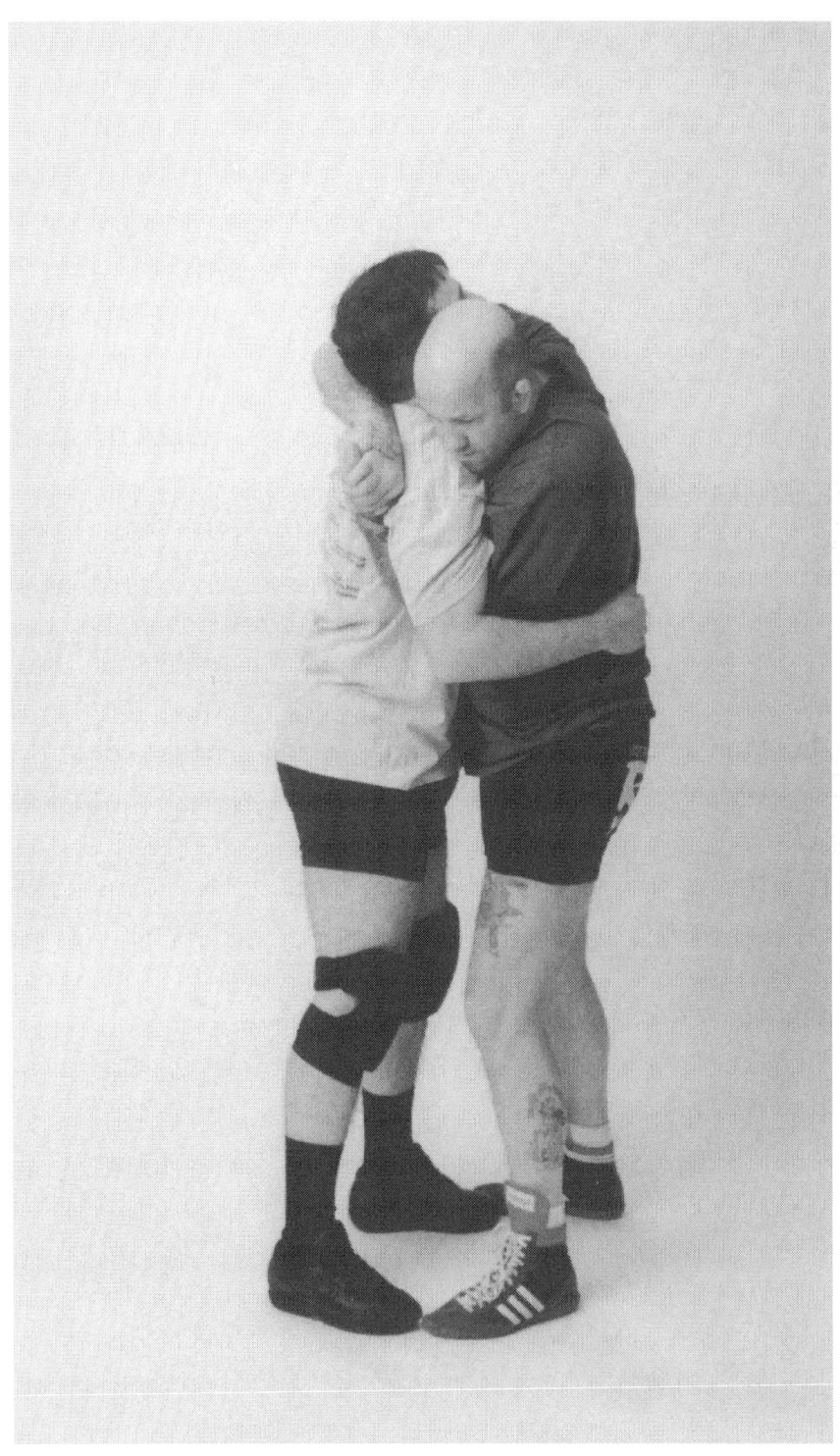

Head and Arm Take-down

Greco-Roman Wrestling

From this same grip you can also take the conventional hip throw (cross buttock) by simply turning in so that your bottom is just past lower abdomen. Lift him over your hip and slam him into the floor.

Head and Arm Take-down

Greco-Roman Wrestling

Conclusion

As I have stated in the other volumes of the throws and take-downs series this is not a comprehensive text on Greco-Roman wrestling. It is not intended to be. I have only learned the art to a level one instructor standard. What I have always managed to do with my training is integrate the solid basics of many styles into one so that it suits me. I would recommend that everyone do this, so that in the end each of us has our own unique style. Don't allow yourself to become a clone, there is nothing worse. What works for one person may be entirely unsuitable for another so mould the technique and make it your own.

What you see here are the techniques I favour most from the Greco system, my best techniques if you like. Certainly they are the ones that I personally find most effective. I hope, if nothing else, that they encourage you to seek out higher instruction in this ancient and highly effective art.

As with anything worth its salt none of the techniques in this book are just going to come to you. You must drill them until they become a part of you, you have to drill them until you

Conclusion

hate them to pieces and you can execute them without having to think. Once you can do this, the technique will be yours. What I like most about the Greco system in particular is the body building qualities. A year of practising with this system will make you very strong, not only in a physical sense but also mentally. Mental toughness is one of the great attributes of most grappling systems.

I hope that this has worked for you and that it will help you to develop such a high level of confidence that you will eventually be able to walk away from violent confrontation and only use your skills should you be forced into a corner. As I have already stated, this book will not make you an expert; I could give you a book on Monet (the painter) but it wouldn't make you a great impressionist. Rather it is the first step in mastering one of the forgotten arts, the art of Greco-Roman wrestling.

Thank you very much for reading and may God bless you.
Geoff Thompson 2001

The Throws and Take-Downs of Sombo

ALSO IN THIS SERIES:

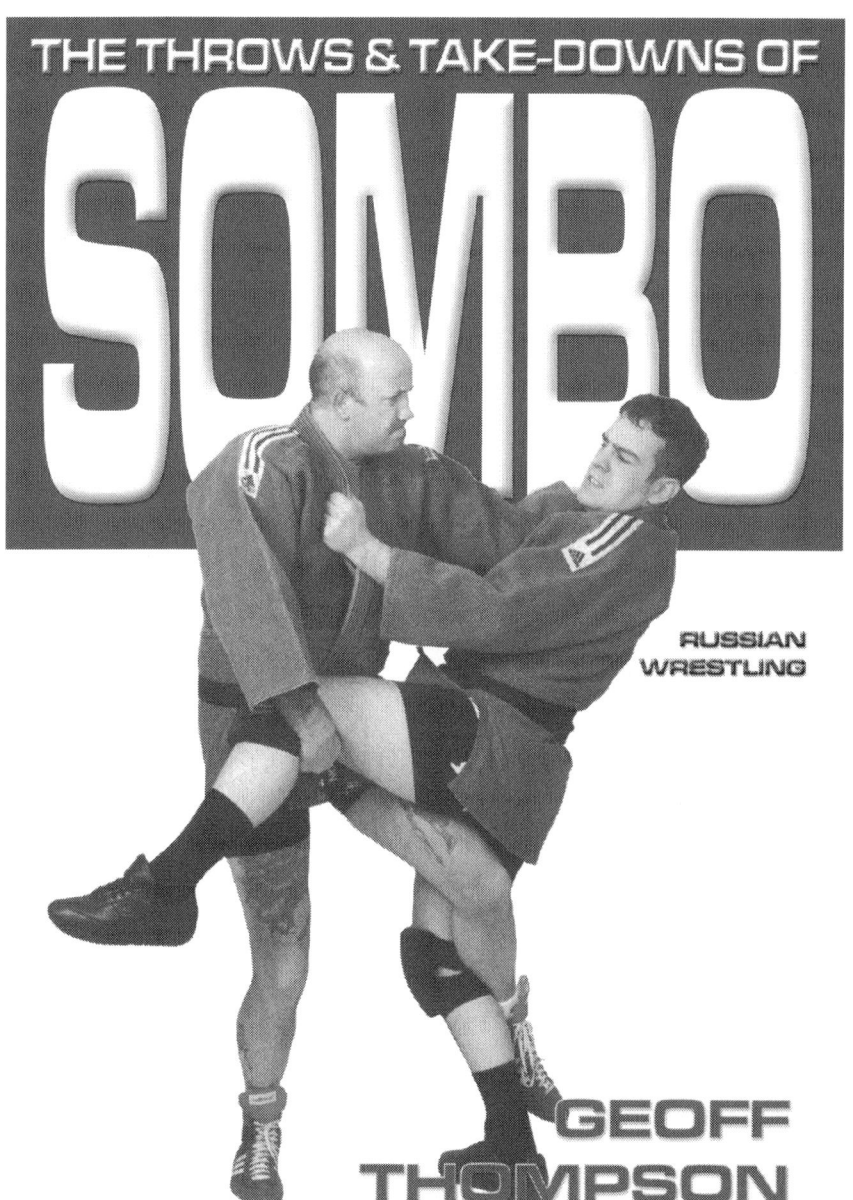

The Throws and Take-Downs of Judo

ALSO IN THIS SERIES:

THE THROWS & TAKE-DOWNS OF JUDO

GEOFF THOMPSON

SUMMERSDALE

The Throws and Take-Downs of Freestyle Wrestling

ALSO IN THIS SERIES:

***Geoff Thompson's autobiography,
Watch My Back***

WATCH MY BACK

GEOFF THOMPSON
WATCH MY BACK

'I train for the first shot – it's all I need.'

'LENNIE MCLEAN HAD THE BRAWN, DAVE COURTNEY HAD THE CHARM, BUT GEOFF THOMPSON IS IN A CLASS OF HIS OWN.' FHM

www.geoffthompson.com

www.summersdale.com